ies
THE W...
e loan
...er.
D0352670

Variation in Living Things

Robert Snedden

WALTHAM FOREST LIBRARIES

904 000 00260438

www.raintreepublishers.co.uk
Visit our website to find out
more information about
Raintree books.

To order:
☎ Phone 0845 6044371
📄 Fax +44 (0) 1865 312263
💻 Email myorders@raintreepublishers.co.uk

Customers from outside the UK please telephone +44 1865 312262

Raintree is an imprint of Capstone Global Library Limited,
a company incorporated in England and Wales having its
registered office at 7 Pilgrim Street, London, EC4V 6LB –
Registered company number: 6695582

Text © Capstone Global Library Limited 2012
First published in hardback in 2012
Paperback edition first published in 2013
The moral rights of the proprietor have been asserted.

All rights reserved. No part of this publication may be
reproduced in any form or by any means (including
photocopying or storing it in any medium by electronic
means and whether or not transiently or incidentally to
some other use of this publication) without the written
permission of the copyright owner, except in accordance
with the provisions of the Copyright, Designs and
Patents Act 1988 or under the terms of a licence
issued by the Copyright Licensing Agency, Saffron
House, 6–10 Kirby Street, London EC1N 8TS (www.cla.
co.uk). Applications for the copyright owner's written
permission should be addressed to the publisher.

Edited by Andrew Farrow, Adrian Vigliano, and
 Diyan Leake
Designed by Victoria Allen
Picture research by Elizabeth Alexander
Illustrations by Oxford Designers & Illustrators
Originated by Capstone Global Library Ltd
Printed in China

ISBN 978 1 406 23256 1 (hardback)
15 14 13 12 11
10 9 8 7 6 5 4 3 2 1

ISBN 978 1 406 23263 9 (paperback)
16 15 14 13 12
10 9 8 7 6 5 4 3 2 1

British Library Cataloguing in Publication Data
Snedden, Robert.
 Variation in living things. -- (The web of life)
 576.5'4-dc22
A full catalogue record for this book is available from
the British Library.

Acknowledgements
The author and publisher are grateful to the following
for permission to reproduce copyright material:
Corbis p. 27 (© Brian J. Skerry/National Geographic
Society); Getty Images p. 41 (Evaristo SA/AFP);
Moorfields communications team p. 39; Photolibrary
pp. 5 (momentimages), 7 (Johann Schumacher), 10
(Javier Larrea), 13 (Dennis Kunkel), 28 (Gilles Martin),
29 (Bildagentur RM), 33 (Roger Eritja), 37 (Pixmann
Limited), 40 (Gary k Smith); Press Association Images p. 6
(Troy Maben); Science Photo Library p. 20 (Oak Ridge
National Laboratory / US Department Of Energy), 23
(Juergen Berger), 22 (Eye of Science), 38 (Philippe Plailly/
Eurelios; Shutterstock pp. 9 (© Mateusz Kopyt), 12 (©
Katie Smith Photography), 17 (© Francois van Heerden),
14 (© Eduard Kyslynskyy), 19 top (© aguilarphoto), 19
bottom (© Denise Kappa), 21 (© HelleM), 24 (© r.nagy),
30 (© Malota), 34 (© Jan Hopgood), 35 (© FotoVeto),
36 (© Ron Hilton), 18 (© Linda Bucklin), 43 (© Valentyn
Volkov), 43 (© Dulce Rubia), 43 (© Monticello), 42
(© Africa Studio), 42 (© Awardimages), 42 (© Zloneg), 42
(© matin), 43 (© Petr Malyshev), 43 (© Piotr Malczyk).

Cover photograph of blond (white) and brown grizzly
bears playfighting reproduced with permission of
Photolibrary/Steven Kazlowski/Peter Arnold Images.

Every effort has been made to contact copyright holders
of material reproduced in this book. Any omissions will
be rectified in subsequent printings if notice is given to
the publisher.

Disclaimer
All the internet addresses (URLs) given in this book were
valid at the time of going to press. However, due to the
dynamic nature of the internet, some addresses may
have changed, or sites may have changed or ceased to
exist since publication. While the author and publisher
regret any inconvenience this may cause readers, no
responsibility for any such changes can be accepted

Waltham Forest Libraries	
904 000 00260438	
Askews & Holts	02-Apr-2013
C576.54 SNE	£8.99
3842367	

Contents

Some words appear in the text in bold, **like this**. You can find out what they mean by looking in the glossary.

The same – but different

It is usually easy to see the differences between the various kinds of plants and animals. For example, a penguin looks very different from an owl, and a tomato looks very different from an oak tree. But how different can one owl be from another owl of the same kind? What differences might there be between one tomato plant and another?

Species

Scientists divide the living world into a number of different groupings of **organisms**. Each member of the group shares certain characteristics. For example, birds are a group of animals that all have feathers – a feature found in no other living things. Birds can be divided up into smaller groups, such as owls and penguins.

The smallest division that can be made is the **species**, such as the tawny owl, or the king penguin. Members of a species can breed together to produce offspring that will also be able to reproduce themselves. Individual members of a species will have many things in common, but they may also be strikingly different.

Variation

The difference between one individual living thing of one species and another of the same species is called variation. Variation applies to all living things, including us. You just have to look at the people around you to see how varied we humans can be.

Differences can matter

Just as some people are taller than others, so some birds in a species will have slightly longer beaks than others. The longer beaked birds might find it easier to get insects out of tree bark, which may mean they eat better than the short beaked birds. This advantage could mean that the longer beaked birds are more likely to raise their young successfully.

Some of the rich variety of the human race can be seen here.

WORD BANK

organism any kind of living thing

species group of living things that have shared characteristics and which can breed together to produce fertile offspring

5

A closer look at species

Although we think of a **species** as being the basic unit of the way we classify living things, there is no accurate definition of what a species actually is. It is true that members of the same species can produce **fertile** offspring together, but in some cases members of different but similar species can also mate and produce fertile offspring.

The grolar bear

Grizzly bears are found in North America, ranging from the northwest United States, through western Canada, and into Alaska. In recent years they have been moving further north and east into areas where polar bears roam. In 2006, the first grolar bear was found – the result of a mating between a male grizzly bear and a female polar bear.

Polar bears and grizzly bears are closely related, but they have always been considered as separate species. The grolar bear is not a new species. It is something called a **hybrid**, which is the result of a cross between two different species. Hybrids are fairly common in nature where the territories of similar species overlap.

This grolar bear had a polar bear mother and a grizzly bear father.

Races

The northern flicker is a type of woodpecker that is found over large areas of North America. There are two distinct varieties of northern flicker. In fact, they are so distinct, that the northern flicker was once thought to be two different species.

In the east, the "yellow-shafted" flicker has distinctive yellow wing feathers. In the west, the "red-shafted" flicker has red wing feathers. Where the two types meet they interbreed freely, producing young with mixed red and yellow feathers.

This example shows how a species can sometimes be divided into smaller groups. These are called **subspecies** and races. They are different from each other, but not different enough to be classed as separate species. Yellow-shafted and red-shafted flickers appear different, but the fact that they breed together so easily points towards them actually being two varieties of the same species.

This bird was once thought to be two distinct species – the yellow-shafted flicker and the red-shafted flicker. It actually is the yellow-shafted variety of the northern flicker.

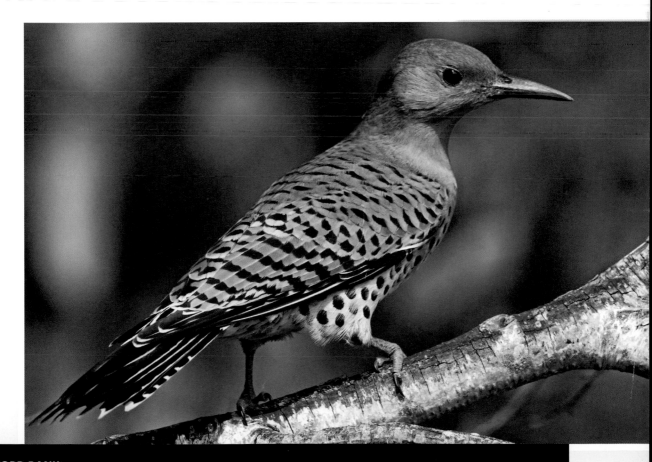

WORD BANK
hybrid   organism that is the offspring of parents from two different species
subspecies   smaller group within a species that has some features that set it apart from other members of the species

Types of variation

There are two types of variation in a species. These are called **continuous variation** and **discontinuous variation**.

Continuous variation

For most variations the individuals in a population show a range of differences. This is known as continuous variation. Height and weight are examples of continuous variation. If you take a group of people, such as a school year group, they will range from the shortest to the tallest, with many possible heights between the two.

The bell curve

If you look at a group of people, you will probably see that most are around the same height; only a few will be either very short or very tall. If you were to measure everyone and plot their heights on a graph, you would get a bell-shaped curve that is highest in the middle and falls off evenly on either side. It shows how variations are distributed in a normal group.

Number of people

Height

Discontinuous variation

For some types of variation, there are only a few possibilities for each characteristic. One obvious example of this is gender, where an **organism** is usually either male or female. (There are exceptions to this. For example, snails, slugs, and earthworms can be both male and female at the same time.) Another example, which we will look at later, is blood group.

Common confusions

Eye colour – continuous or discontinuous?

Sometimes eye colour is described as an example of discontinuous variation. This is because people think of eyes as being brown, or blue, or green, and so on. However, although there may be many people with brown eyes, for example, there can be many different shades of brown. Eye colour can range from very dark, almost black, to very pale blue, with endless variety between the two extremes. Therefore eye colour is an example of continuous variation.

Can you curl your tongue? Some people can and some can't. This is an example of discontinuous variation.

WORD BANK

continuous variation   variation that takes place over a range of measurements, for example height and weight

discontinuous variation   variation in which there are only a few distinct varieties, with nothing in between, for example blood groups

Gener tion to gener tion

Living things always develop in a similar way to the parents that produced them. A pig will never give birth to a puppy, a goose won't hatch from a seagull's egg, and an apple tree won't grow from a grass seed. This might seem obvious, but why should it be?

Genes

All living things are made of **cells**, the smallest units of life. Everything began life as a single cell that divided again and again until it became a fully formed **organism**. Each cell contains the information needed to control this process. This information is stored in the cell in the form of **genes**.

You might think of genes as being instructions for the different characteristics that each living thing has. For example, genes control the colour of your eyes and the way your body responds to different diseases.

WHAT IT MEANS FOR US

Understanding how genes work has given modern scientists the means to produce crops that have many beneficial characteristics. For instance, they can have a greater resistance to disease and drought, and greater yield of fruits and seeds. Plants can be grown from single cells in a laboratory, making the process of producing new varieties much faster.

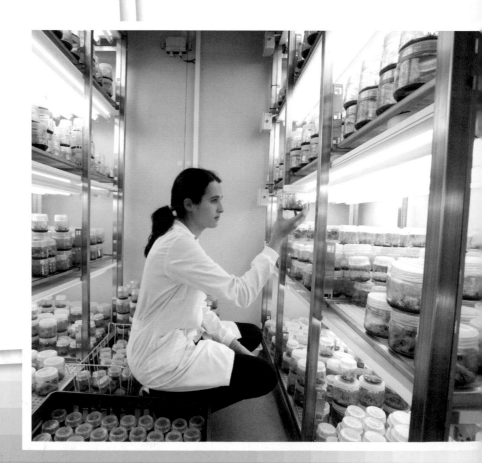

Patterns of inheritance

It was an Austrian monk called Gregor Mendel (1822–1884) who began to make the first discoveries about genes. He made a study of the way characteristics were passed from one generation of pea plants to the next. From his observations he set out two laws of **heredity**, the process by which genes are passed from one generation to the next:

- The first law said that each characteristic was determined by a separate hereditary unit. We now call them genes. The genes were found in pairs, one coming from the mother and one from the father.

- The second law, which we will explore later, says that different characteristics can be **inherited** independently of one another. For example, a pea plant could be tall with white flowers or short with white flowers. Its height did not affect its flower colour.

Today we know that Mendel was right in many respects – but he didn't know the whole story. Several genes acting together control some characteristics, and sometimes characteristics can be linked to each other.

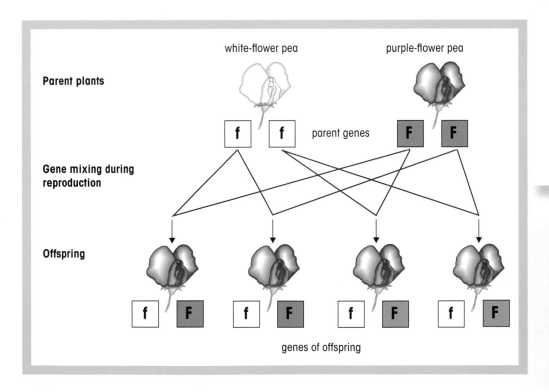

white-flower pea   purple-flower pea

Parent plants

f   f   parent genes   F   F

Gene mixing during reproduction

Offspring

f F   f F   f F   f F

genes of offspring

For each characteristic, one of each pair of genes is inherited from each parent.

WORD BANK
heredity the transfer of characteristics from parents to their offspring
inherit receive from the previous generation

Variation and inheritance

You've probably noticed the way people sometimes look at children and remark at how much they look like their parents. This is because many of the variations we see in living things are passed on from one generation to the next.

Genetic variation

Each new living thing will have features in common with both parents because the genes it has will have come from them. Yet the new living thing will be different from either of its parents because it has a new combination of genes. Whenever **fertilization** takes place, whether in animals or in plants, a unique set of genes is created. This recombining of genes is one of the things that give rise to variation.

Common confusions

Are identical twins really identical?

Identical twins used to be regarded as an exception to the rule that no living things have the same genes. Because they developed from a single fertilized egg, it was believed that they would have exactly the same set of genes. Researchers have discovered recently that this isn't quite true. There are some differences, and these can be important. For example, one twin might have leukaemia (a type of cancer that affects the blood), while the other one doesn't.

Genome

All of the information needed to build and maintain a living organism is coded into its genes. The complete set of genes carried by an organism is called its **genome**. Each member of a species has a very similar genome. The giraffe genome is a set of instructions for making a giraffe, the birch tree genome makes a birch tree, and, of course, the human genome makes humans.

Small differences

Ninety-nine point nine per cent of the human genome is identical from one person to the next. It is just that 0.1 per cent that is unique that helps to make us all different individuals.

WHAT IT MEANS FOR US

By mapping the human genome, scientists have made great advances in discovering how differences in our genomes can have a big effect on health. For example, a drug that can help one patient can be harmful to another because of differences in their genes. Statins, used to lower cholesterol, can cause weakening of the muscles in people with a particular gene.

Sickle cell anaemia is an inherited illness in which some of the red blood cells do not form properly.

WORD BANK
fertilization   when a sperm cell joins with an egg to make a new cell with two genomes
genome   all of the genetic information held in the cells of an organism

Dominant and recessive genes

We don't actually have a single genome – we have two. Each of our parents gives us one complete set of genes. When fertilization takes place, a sperm cell (which has one copy of the genome) joins with an egg (which has another copy) to make a new cell with two genomes.

Alleles

The two copies of a particular gene are called **alleles**. The particular combination of alleles found in each individual is another of the factors that go towards making us all unique. In one of Mendel's experiments, he crossed pea plants that always had purple flowers with pea plants that always had white flowers. He discovered that all the plants resulting from this cross had purple flowers.

In the purple-flowered plants, the alleles for flower colour were both for purple. In the white-flowered plants, they were both for white. When the plants were crossed, the offspring got one purple allele and one white allele – yet the result was that they were all purple. Why should this be?

The unusual colouring of a white tiger is the result of a recessive gene.

The allele for purple flowers is the one that determines the colour of the flowers. It is said to be **dominant** over the allele for white flowers, which is said to be **recessive**. White flowers only appear in plants that have two white alleles. Where there is also a purple allele present, it masks the effect of the white allele.

Genome and genotype

The combined effect of the genomes, determined by which of the alleles is dominant and which recessive, results in the organism's **genotype**. While the genome is all of the organism's genes, the genotype is the actual effect these genes have on the organism's development.

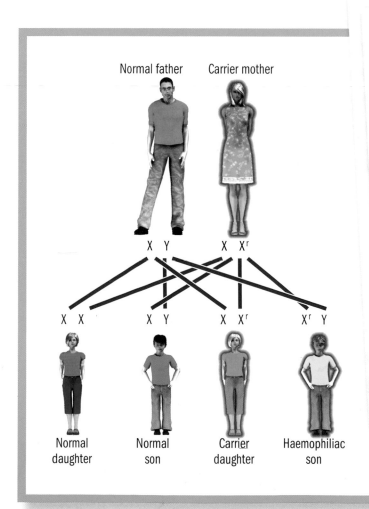

Normal father   Carrier mother

X Y   X X^r

X X   X Y   X X^r X^r Y

Normal   Normal   Carrier   Haemophiliac
daughter   son   daughter   son

WHAT IT MEANS FOR US

Dominant and recessive genes can be very important for us, especially where genetic illnesses are concerned. Haemophilia is a disease in which the blood does not clot efficiently. This means that even a small wound can be serious. Haemophilia is caused by a faulty gene. Boys only have one copy of the gene in question, and if it is a faulty one the disease becomes apparent. Girls are protected by having a dominant working copy of the gene, but they can be carriers of the disease and run the risk of passing it on to their sons.

WORD BANK
allele one of a pair of alternative forms of a gene
dominant gene allele that determines the appearance, or phenotype, of the organism

Independent assortment

In his first experiments with peas, Gregor Mendel was looking at single characteristics, such as whether the flowers were white or purple, whether the seeds were round or wrinkled, or whether the plants were tall or short. Then he began to look at what happened when the parents differed by more than one characteristic – for example, tall plants with purple flowers and short plants with white flowers.

Multiplying differences

It is easier to see what Mendel discovered by looking at a diagram. Capital letters are used to show dominant alleles, and lower case letters to show recessive alleles. Suppose we have one plant with alleles AABB and another with alleles aabb of the A and B genes. These genes control height (A) and flower colour (B). The diagram below shows all the 16 possible combinations that can arise from just these two genes. As you can see, only one combination produces a short plant with white flowers.

Crossing two characteristics

Key		AB	Ab	aB	ab
☐ alleles from parent 1					
◼ alleles from parent 2	AB	AABB	AABb	AaBB	AaBb
☐ tall with purple flowers	Ab	AABb	AAbb	AaBb	AAbb
◼ tall with white flowers	aB	AaBB	AaBb	aaBB	aaBb
☐ short with purple flowers	ab	AaBb	AAbb	aaBb	aabb
☐ short with white flowers					

The more gene pairs we look at, the more the possible combinations start to multiply enormously. For parents differing by 10 genes there are almost 60,000 possible combinations in their offspring. If there are 20 different pairs the number leaps to nearly 3.5 billion. Now consider that there are around 20,000 genes in the human genome and you will begin to see just how unique we all are.

Here we see the variety that just two genes can bring. The B gene determines eye colour (B dominant = brown eyes, b recessive = blue eyes) and the Y gene determines either curly hair (Y dominant) or straight hair (y recessive). So in this example, a person has to have bbyy genes to have blue eyes and straight hair.

WHAT IT MEANS FOR US

The vast number of possible gene combinations in humans is what makes **genetic fingerprinting** possible. Analysing just a tiny amount of material from a person's body, such as a drop of blood, is enough to distinguish them from any other person. This technique can be used to identify people who have died in natural disasters, allowing people to know what has happened to friends or family members who have gone missing.

Cheetahs have very little genetic variety. The present-day cheetah population is thought to be descended from only a small number of ancestors.

Variation and environment

Genes obviously play a major role in determining how an **organism** looks, but they are not the only factor. The **environment** has a part to play, too.

Genotype and phenotype

As we have seen, the information held in a living thing's genes make up its **genotype**. The genotype is the set of instructions for making and maintaining a living thing. Until the instructions are followed, there is no living thing to see.

The actual appearance of the organism produced by following the instructions in the genotype is called its **phenotype**. The phenotype is the physical appearance of the organism – everything that makes it up. If you think of the genotype as being like the blueprint for a building, then the phenotype is the actual place you can walk into.

Environmental factors are important in the way the phenotype is built from the genotype. It is all very well having instructions to make a tall plant, for example, but if there is a shortage of water or **nutrients** in the soil, the plant will not grow as tall as it might.

Your genotype is the plan for building and running your body. Just how that plan is carried out will depend on other factors, such as your diet and the amount of exercise you get.

Changing colours

Many gardeners will know of one particular way that changes in the environment can have an effect on the appearance of a plant. The hydrangea is a popular garden shrub with flowers that can be shades of pink and blue. The colour of the flowers depends on how acid the soil is. The flowers are blue in acid soil conditions, mauve in acid to neutral soil conditions, and pink in alkaline conditions. So the hydrangea is a good indicator of soil conditions, helping the gardener to decide what other plants will grow well there.

WORD BANK
environment   all of the living and non-living things that surround an organism
phenotype   appearance of an organism resulting from the interaction between its genes and the environment

Were you born that way?

For centuries, people have debated whether genetics or the environment are more important in deciding how we are. This is often referred to as the "nature versus **nurture**" debate. For example, are some people more likely to put on weight than others? Or is this something that could happen to anyone who eats an unhealthy diet and doesn't exercise enough – regardless of their genes?

A growing problem

In 2009, nearly a quarter of adults in England were obese. Around one in six boys and one in seven girls aged from 2 to 15 were obese. These numbers are predicted to increase. Being overweight can lead to health problems, such as heart disease, so it is a serious issue.

Genes and obesity

So far, more than 200 genes have been identified that are involved in some way in body weight and in fat storage in the body. One of these is called the FTO gene. However, it is not found in everyone, and is most common in people of European descent. The people who have this gene are likely to be an average of 2–3 kilograms (4½–6½ pounds) heavier than those who don't, and to be more at risk of becoming **obese**.

However, a person who carries this gene is not necessarily doomed to become obese. We can make choices about our lifestyles that can counteract the effect of the genes.

The mouse on the left has a **mutated** form of a gene that has caused it to gain more weight than the normal mouse on the right.

WHAT IT MEANS FOR US

Although genes can obviously play a part in determining body weight, environmental factors come into play as well. Many people have jobs that involve sitting at a desk all day. Often they will drive to and from work, and when they get back home may spend the evening sitting in front of the television. The lack of exercise means that they are not using up enough of the energy they get from the food they eat. The body will simply store the excess, and the result is weight gain.

By making a positive choice to eat healthy food and not to overeat, and also to take exercise regularly, most people should be able to control their weight.

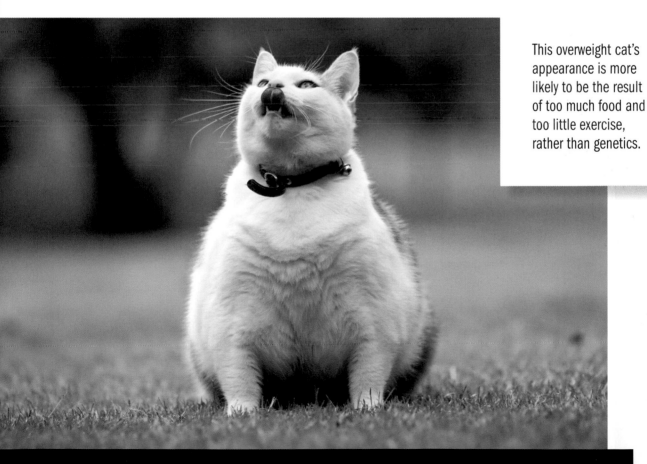

This overweight cat's appearance is more likely to be the result of too much food and too little exercise, rather than genetics.

WORD BANK
nurture all the environmental factors that influence the behaviour and traits of an organism
obese so overweight that health is endangered

Mutations

Because of the huge number of different ways in which genes can combine from one generation to the next, there would seem to be almost endless possibilities for variation. But this is just shuffling the genetic pack of cards to make new combinations of genes that already exist. We need to be able to explain why sometimes variations appear that have never been seen before.

When a cell divides, its genes are copied so each new cell has a complete set of genes. Every once in a while, a mistake might be made when this copying is done, and a gene will be produced that is different. These changed genes are called **mutations**. As well as resulting from random copying errors, mutations can also be caused by environmental factors, such as radiation and chemicals.

Most mutations are harmful. They interfere with the proper functions of the cell, and as a result it may die. Sometimes a mutated cell survives – but because it is only one among billions in the body, it has no obvious effect on the **organism**.

A mutation has made legs grow where this fruit fly's antennae should be.

To the next generation

Mutations that happen in egg or sperm cells affect the whole organism because they will be copied into every one of its cells as it develops. The mutation might have no effect at all; or it might have such a small effect that it causes no advantage or disadvantage. Mutations that result in the death of the organism are called lethals.

A few mutations can be of real benefit to an organism. For example, some mutations can give insects the ability to resist the effects of insecticides. Insects with this mutation are the ones that will survive and reproduce, which means growing populations of insects that are harder to control.

WHAT IT MEANS FOR US

MRSA (yellow in image below) is a type of bacteria that has become very hard to treat. It can cause serious infections, particularly in people who are already unwell, and can be a major problem in hospitals. MRSA was the result of some bacteria having a mutation that made them resistant to the **antibiotics** used to treat them.

Tiny round MRSA bacteria are shown here clinging to fine hair-like structures inside the nose. MRSA is very common on the human body and usually harmless to healthy people.

WORD BANK
mutation   gene that has undergone change
antibiotic   drug used to fight infections caused by bacteria

Variation and evolution

The random variations that result from **mutations** are an important part of the way **species** change and adapt over time. Mutations introduce new variety into a species. Although often these changes will be harmful, sometimes they will give the species more chances to survive in changing conditions.

The fight for survival

No matter how successful an **organism** might be, it is still going to come up against challenges to its survival. Being too successful can cause problems if the organism runs out of room to grow, or food to eat. The members of the species will find themselves in competition for the resources they need to survive.

We have already seen how the members of a species are all very similar genetically, but that there is also variety in their **genes** that results in a range of characteristics. The organisms that are best equipped to survive in their **environment** are the ones most likely to reproduce. They will pass their genes to their offspring, making them better equipped to survive, too.

Natural selection

The process by which genes that give an organism an advantage are selected over those that don't is called natural selection. It is an idea that was first put forward by British naturalist Charles Darwin, and independently by Alfred Russel Wallace, in the 19th century.

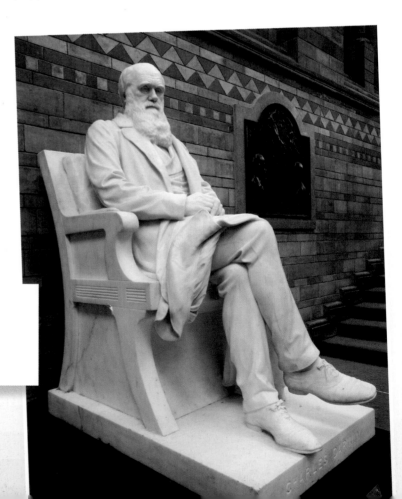

The statue of Charles Darwin in the Natural History Museum, London.

Both men realized that every living thing is in competition for resources. Within a species there is a wide diversity of individuals, and this is what gives the species the potential to **evolve**. Some individuals will have advantages over others and will be more likely to reproduce. However small the advantage might be, over time it will be selected in favour of less advantageous characteristics in the species.

Natural selection comes about as a result of variation and environmental pressures. The organisms best suited to the environment become more numerous than those that aren't. This is sometimes called the "survival of the fittest".

Independent thinking

It is not unusual for different people to have the same idea at around the same time, like Darwin and Wallace. In the 1930s, the turbojet engine was invented by Frank Whittle in Britain and Hans von Ohain in Germany – completely independently of each other!

Beetle population contains both red and blue beetles

Birds eat more of the red beetles than the blue beetles

More blue beetles survive than red ones

In this simple example of natural selection at work, there are two similar species of beetle – one red and one blue. If birds find red beetles tastier or easier to catch than blue beetles, then over time there will be many more blue beetles than red ones. In other words, natural selection favours blue beetles.

Adaptations

The features that arise through natural selection and evolution are called **adaptations**. An adaptation is something that gives a living thing an advantage in its environment. For example, the gills of a fish are adaptations that allow it to breathe in water, and the long tongue of a butterfly lets it get nectar from deep inside a flower.

New species

When Darwin was a young man, he travelled to the Galapagos Islands in the Pacific Ocean. There he discovered what has become one of the most famous examples of the way new species appear.

There are several species of finch on the Galapagos Islands. They are all similar but each has a particular adaptation. For example, one has a slender bill that is good for probing for insects, while another has a strong bill that is good for cracking seeds. All of these different species started out as a single species that arrived on the Galapagos from the mainland. However, there were no other birds on the islands to compete with them.

Natural variation within the ancestor of the Galapagos finches eventually gave rise to all the different species found on the islands today, as the birds exploited the variety of foods available to them.

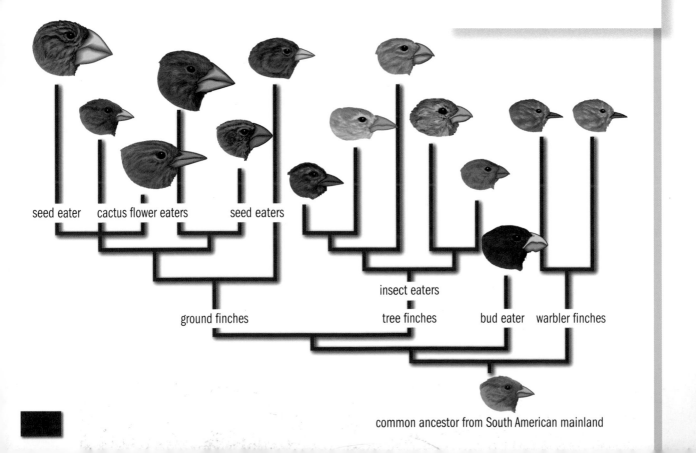

seed eater   cactus flower eaters   seed eaters

insect eaters

ground finches   tree finches   bud eater   warbler finches

common ancestor from South American mainland

Over time, the birds became more specialized and adapted to different types of food. Variation within the original species meant that some birds developed slightly longer and more slender bills and others had slightly thicker and heavier bills. Eventually the different types became so different from the original ancestor birds that they no longer bred with each other. They became new, separate species.

The end of the line

No species lasts forever. One species inevitably gives way to another that is better adapted to changing environmental conditions. A species can become so highly specialized that it no longer has the range of variations needed to adapt. The moist skin of amphibians is an adaptation that allows them to absorb oxygen both in and out of the water. But it also makes them very vulnerable to harmful pollution in the air and in the water. The vast majority of all the species that ever existed are now **extinct**.

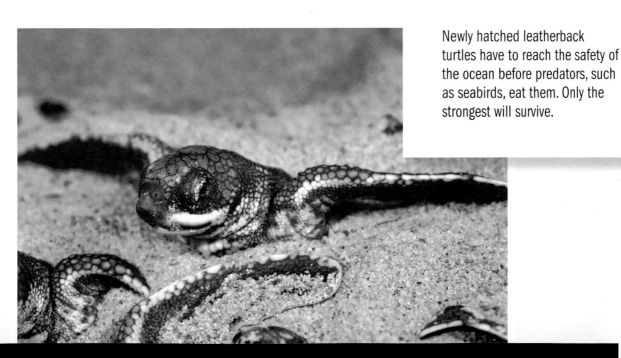

Newly hatched leatherback turtles have to reach the safety of the ocean before predators, such as seabirds, eat them. Only the strongest will survive.

WORD BANK
adaptation feature of a living thing that makes it suited to its environment
extinct describes a species that no longer exists after the last member of the species has died

CASE STUDY

Cuckoo in the nest

The common cuckoo of Europe is an unusual kind of bird, and a fascinating example of **discontinuous variation**. It does not build a nest of its own. Instead it has become adapted to lay its eggs in the nests of other birds. To avoid detection, the cuckoo lays an egg that **mimics** the colouring of the unwitting host bird's eggs.

Matching pairs

There is a type of discontinuous variation among female cuckoos that is not apparent until they lay their eggs. Each different type of female cuckoo is matched up to a particular host bird and will only lay eggs that mimic the eggs of that bird. For example, a cuckoo that lays its eggs in a reed warbler's nest will produce eggs that look like the reed warbler's eggs; and a cuckoo that lays eggs in meadow pipit's nest will have eggs that look like those of the meadow pipit. The "reed warbler" cuckoo cannot switch to being a "meadow pipit" cuckoo.

The cuckoo's egg is larger than the reed warbler's, but the markings are similar enough to fool the reed warblers.

Survival tactics

When the cuckoo chick hatches, it immediately sets to work pushing the host bird's eggs, or any chicks that have hatched, out of the nest. Once it has the nest to itself, it tricks its foster parents into feeding it. The cuckoo chick has an extraordinary begging call, described as sounding like "a whole brood of hungry chicks". The host birds respond to this by working hard to feed the one cuckoo chick.

From mother to daughter

A female cuckoo chick successfully raised in a reed warbler's nest will grow up to be a reed warbler specialist, like its mother. The **genes** that determine the type of eggs laid by the cuckoo are only passed down the female line. The female can breed with any male cuckoo and this will have no effect on the type of eggs she lays.

Catching out the cuckoo

Some birds have **evolved** strategies to catch out the cuckoo. The male reed warbler guards the nest when his mate begins laying her eggs. If the cuckoo does manage to lay an egg in the nest, the reed warblers are more likely to reject it if they have seen the cuckoo near by.

The cuckoo chick soon grows to be bigger than the reed warblers that feed it.

Blood groups

Humans are divided up into different blood groups – another type of **discontinuous variation** that is a result of evolution in humans and their ancestors.

ABO blood group

The most common of the blood groups is called the ABO group. It can be divided into A, B, AB, and O blood types. The different types refer to differences between each person's red blood **cells**. A person can only be one particular type. It is not possible to be a mixture of different types.

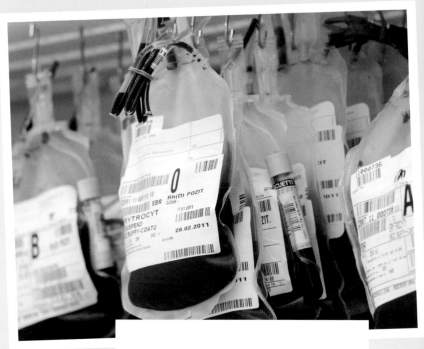

Blood bags are carefully labelled. Giving the wrong type of blood to someone could be disastrous.

Blood transfusion

Hospitals keep supplies of blood for use during surgery or to replace blood lost by accident victims. Blood for transfusions is stored in places called blood banks. The blood can only be kept for a short time and so supplies must be topped up all the time. This is why volunteer blood donors are so vital.

A person can't be given just anyone's blood. Before a blood transfusion can be given to someone, their blood type has to be determined. If the wrong type of blood is given, the body's immune system will attack the new blood cells and destroy them. This means, for example, that a person with type A blood can only receive blood from a type A donor.

The rhesus factor

As well the ABO types, there is also the **rhesus (Rh) factor**. There are two Rh blood groups. A person can be either type Rh positive or type Rh negative. This refers to the presence or absence of features on the red blood cells. Someone with blood type O who is Rh negative is referred to as being "O negative".

This chart shows how complex it is to match blood donors to recipients. Many factors need to be considered. Plasma is the liquid that blood cells are found in.

Blood type of recipient	Donor		
	Whole blood	**Red cells**	**Plasma**
O+	O+ or O-	O+ or O-	O+, O-, A+, A-, B+, B-, AB+, or AB-
O-	O-	O-	O+, O-, A+, A-, B+, B-, AB+, or AB-
A+	A+ or A-	O+, O-, A+, or A-,	A+, A-, AB+, or AB-
A-	A-	A- or O-	A+, A-, AB+, or AB-
B+	B+ or B-	O+, O-, B+, or B-	B+, B-, AB+, or AB-
B-	B-	O- or B-	B+, B-, AB+, or AB-
AB+	AB+ or AB-	O+, O-, A+, A-, B+, B-, AB+, or AB-	AB+ or AB-
AB-	AB -	O-, A-, B-, or AB-	AB+ or AB-

WHAT IT MEANS FOR US

People with type O blood are sometimes referred to as universal donors. The reason for this is that they can safely donate blood to anyone in the ABO group. However, they themselves can only receive blood from type O donors. People who are AB, on the other hand, can receive blood from people of any type.

WORD BANK

rhesus (Rh) factor   a feature of red blood cells that may be present in some people (rhesus positive) and not in others (rhesus negative)

Insect societies

Some insects, such as termites, ants, and some types of wasps and bees, live together in large colonies. These insects are referred to as social insects because they form large societies of many individuals divided into different types, each with a task to perform.

Castes

There are generally three types, or castes, of insect within a colony. These are queens, workers, and males. Some workers may be larger than the others. They are the colony's soldiers and their job is to defend it against attack from threats, such as insects from different colonies. All of the workers are females.

New colonies

Once a year the insect colony produces a new generation of queens and males. Worker ants and termites are wingless; it is only the new queens and the males that can fly. They leave the colony to mate with ants from other colonies. After mating the males die – their only job within the colony is completed. The queen looks for a suitable place to lay her eggs, and so begin a new colony.

Nature and nurture again

Whether an ant will become a queen or a worker is determined by its **genes** and by the **environment**. Researchers studied the Florida harvester ant and discovered that the descendants of some males were more likely to become queens, while those of other males were likely to be workers.

The researchers also investigated the role played by the ants' diet. It appeared that the ant **larvae** that became queens had a diet made up of other animals, while the worker ants had a more plant-based diet. So, both nature (in the form of the ant's genes) and **nurture** (in the form of diet) play a part. Exactly how the two work together is not certain.

Megacolony

Social insects, such as ants and bees, will attack intruders from other colonies. Scientists recently discovered a vast megacolony of Argentine ants that stretches around the world. Originating in South America, the ants have been carried unwittingly from continent to continent by humans. One supercolony of ants is believed to extend 6,000 kilometres around the Mediterranean coast of Europe. Ants from the European supercolony introduced to ants from the Japan supercolony won't fight, proving that they are related.

Worker ants escort winged males from the nest.

WORD BANK
larva (plural: **larvae**)   young form of insects; a maggot is a larva of a fly

Artificial variation

Throughout history, humans have looked for ways to introduce new varieties into living things. For example, we have selected crops that are pest-resistant and give high yields, and plant them in preference to less hardy or productive plants.

Selective breeding

Selective breeding, or artificial selection, is the process of deliberately breeding plants and animals to produce offspring with characteristics that we find useful. For example, farmers want to have cows that yield the most milk, or chickens that lay the most eggs. By continually selecting and breeding from only the individuals that produce the most milk or eggs, there will eventually be new varieties of a **species** that have the characteristics we want.

A variety, also called a **breed**, will have characteristics that set it apart – but it is not a new species. Any variety of a species can breed with any other variety. There are a great many cattle breeds, such as the Holstein cow, which is a good milk producer, and the Aberdeen Angus, which is prized for the quality of its beef.

Plant breeders have grown many different varieties of pepper, from sweet bell peppers to hot chillies. All of them belong to the same species.

The gene pool

A **gene** pool is all of the genes present within a species – not just the genes found in a single individual. The greater the variety of genes within the species, the more adaptable it is likely to be. By breeding plants and animals to have certain characteristics, we are reducing the size of their gene pool by rejecting the features we don't want.

WHAT IT MEANS FOR US

Natural selection results in living things that are best suited to their **environment**. Artificial selection produces living things that are best suited for our purposes. However, this can cause problems. For example, if all the members of a breed are genetically very similar, we are actually reducing the variety within that breed. Also, by selecting only the characteristics we want, we may be producing plants and animals that are more vulnerable to new diseases.

For thousands of years, people have kept pigs. There are now more than 300 breeds. However, wild boars like this one were the ancestors of all our domestic pigs.

WORD BANK

breed group of domestic animals with characteristics that distinguish them from other members of the same species

From wolf to dog

One of the most startling examples of people producing new breeds within a single species is in the huge variety of shapes, sizes, and characteristics we can see in domestic dogs. From tiny Chihuahuas to large and powerful mastiffs, all of these animals belong to a single species – and all of the differences between them are a result of selective breeding.

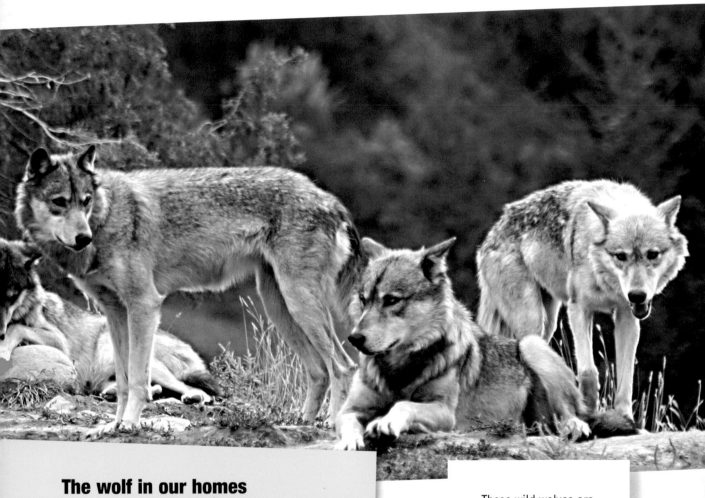

The wolf in our homes

It has long been thought that dogs are descended from wolves, but it is only in recent years that scientists have been able to prove this. Researchers compared the **genomes** of dogs and grey wolves, and discovered a difference of only 0.2 per cent. This shows there is a very close link between the two animals.

These wild wolves are very closely related to the dogs that share many of our homes.

The origins of the dog

The best guess at the moment when dogs were first domesticated is around 15,000 years ago. Where this took place is also uncertain. There is some evidence to suggest it happened in East Asia, but it also seems likely that some breeds of dog started out in the Middle East and Africa. The likeliest explanation is that wolves were domesticated in several different places at around the same time.

The modern dog

Most of the dog breeds we are familiar with today have been developed over the last 200 years by breeders, who have carefully selected dogs with the desired characteristics. Careful records, called pedigrees, are kept of breeding to ensure that the character of the dog is maintained.

The German shepherd dog, for example, originated from mountain sheepdogs that were bred by Captain Max von Stephanitz at the end of the 19th century. He selected dogs that were strong and intelligent to work as herding dogs. The German shepherd became popular as a working dog for a number of activities, including police work.

It may be hard to imagine that the wide variety of domestic dogs are all descended from wolves, but they are.

Genetic engineering

While we can use selective breeding to change the characteristics of plants and animals over generations, **genetic engineering** allows us to change them in a single step. And whereas selective breeding is only carried out within a species, with genetic engineering we can take genes from one species and add them to another.

This ram has been genetically engineered to produce genes that can be used to treat human genetic illnesses.

Designer plants

Plants can be genetically engineered to be resistant to powerful chemicals that are used to kill weeds. Genetically modified (GM) soya beans were one of the first crops to be modified in this way. In 1994 the first GM plant to be approved for human consumption was a tomato that had been genetically altered to ripen more slowly. This increased the amount of time the tomatoes could stay on the supermarket shelf.

Another plant developed by genetic engineering was golden rice. A carrot gene was inserted into the rice plant so that it would produce more vitamin A. The idea behind this was that people's diets could be improved by eating the golden rice.

Questions to think about

Many people welcomed the development of golden rice and its higher vitamin A content. Around 400 million people worldwide suffer from vitamin A deficiency in their diet. It is a problem in large areas of Africa, India, and elsewhere in Asia. The **World Health Organization** estimates that 500,000 children a year go blind because of lack of vitamin A.

However, environmental campaigners have fought against the introduction of golden rice. One argument against it is that it will have an effect on the variety of food crops that are grown. If people rely on the golden rice, they might no longer grow other plants, leading to a loss of **biodiversity**. What do you think of these two opposing views?

WHAT IT MEANS FOR US

Human genes have also been used in genetic engineering. Cystic fibrosis is a common genetic disease that attacks the lungs and digestive system. It is an incurable condition caused by a faulty gene that fails to produce a **protein** that the body needs. By inserting a good copy of the gene into sheep, they can be made to produce the missing protein in their milk. This can then be extracted and used to treat the cystic fibrosis sufferer.

Consultant surgeon James Bainbridge headed a team at Moorfields Eye Hospital, London, successfully treating an **inherited** eye condition using gene therapy.

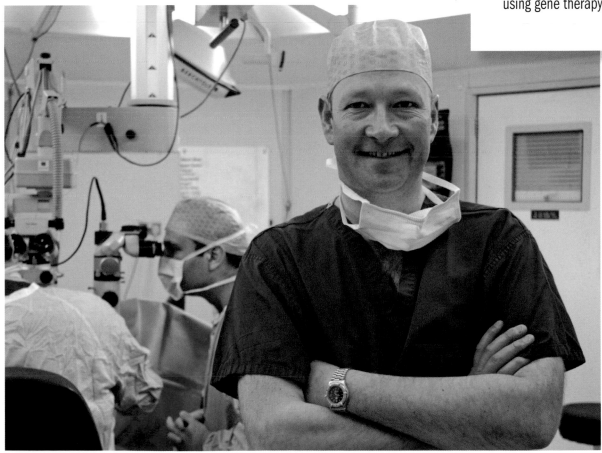

WORD BANK
genetic engineering deliberately changing the genes of an organism in the laboratory
biodiversity variety of different living things found in a place

39

Clones

Clones are organisms that are genetically identical. Any differences between one clone and another will be the result of environmental factors. There are many examples of clones in nature. Strawberry plants that grow from runners, rather than seeds, are genetically identical to the parent plant. Gardeners and plant breeders will often produce new plants by taking cuttings from a plant. The plants that grow from the cuttings are clones of the original plant.

A strawberry plant spreads by producing offshoots called runners. The new plant is genetically identical to the parent.

WHAT IT MEANS FOR US

One suggestion for the use of cloned animals is in the mass production of animals engineered to carry human genes, such as the sheep used in the treatment of cystic fibrosis. Another possibility is the creation of genetically modified pigs that could produce organs suitable for human transplants.

Clone research

In 1997, researchers in Scotland successfully produced the world's first cloned mammal, an event that would never happen in nature. This was Dolly the sheep. Scientists cloned Dolly by taking the genetic material from a donor sheep cell and inserting it into another cell from which the genetic material had been removed. The new cell was made to begin dividing in the laboratory. When it was successfully growing, it was implanted into the womb of a female sheep where it continued to develop until birth.

The problems with cloning

Cloning of animals is difficult and expensive to achieve. Over 90 per cent of attempts fail to produce offspring that survive. Research has shown also that those that do survive may have poor health and die early for mysterious reasons. Scientists suspect that part of the reason may be that the cloned animal's genes are not working properly.

Cloning and variation

Another disadvantage to cloning is that it works against variation. To clone a whole herd of cows with especially high milk yields might seem like a good idea – but there would be huge risks. Cloning reduces the gene pool to its minimum. All the animals in the cloned herd would be identical, with identical immune systems. If the herd was struck by disease, either all of them would live – or all of them would die.

No doubt there is a place for artificial cloning, but we would be very short sighted if we failed to safeguard the amazing variety in the world.

Common confusions

Cloning and genetic engineering

Although they are often thought of together, cloning is not a form of genetic engineering. When an organism is cloned, the genes of the parent **organism** are not changed in any way. If they were, the offspring would be genetically different from its parent, and therefore not a clone.

This cow was the first cloned animal in Latin America. Her calf was born in September 2004, through natural reproduction, and scientists say her growth is normal.

Food variety

Have you ever wondered about the huge variety of fruit and vegetables that we have to choose from today? Have you noticed all the different types of apples and potatoes? You might not know that the fruit and vegetables we eat today have changed a lot from the ones that were being eaten thousands of years ago, when there was much less variety. Growers have produced a huge range of variations in food plants over the centuries.

Potatoes

Did you know that there are around 5,000 varieties of potato worldwide? Three thousand of them are only found in the Andes Mountains of South America, where they were first grown by farmers over 7,000 years ago.

Sweetcorn

The ancestor of sweetcorn, called teosinte, had just five to twelve little **kernels**, each one held inside a hard shell.

Kiwi fruit

The kiwi fruit was originally a hard berry that grew in China. Plant breeders in New Zealand developed the soft green fruit eaten today.

Tomatoes

Tomatoes grown today can weigh a thousand times as much as their wild ancestors, which were small green fruits first grown in South America. Today there are thousands of varieties of tomato, some with amusing names such as Alberto Shatters, Butter 'n' Eggs, Green Zebra, and Little Willie's Mouthful.

Cabbage

All the varieties of cabbage, Brussels sprouts, broccoli, and cauliflower we eat today were developed from a single wild ancestor – the wild cabbage, or wild mustard plant.

Carrots

Carrots originally came in a wide variety of colours, including red, yellow, and even purple. The orange carrots we are familiar with today were developed in the Netherlands in the seventeenth century.

Wheat

Wheat, a type of grass, was first grown over 10,000 years ago. The first farmers selected mutant varieties that had large grains that were firmly attached to the stalks. The result was the development of a plant that couldn't survive in the wild because it could no longer disperse its seeds.

Aubergines

Aubergines are not just large, oval-shaped, dark-purple vegetables. Many different varieties are grown in parts of Asia. They can be reddish purple, white, yellow, or green. They can be small and round, long and slim, or weigh up to a kilogram.

Apples

The wild ancestor of the apple grows in Central Asia. The name of the city of Alma-ata in Kazakhstan means "Grandfather of Apples". Today, more than 7,500 varieties of apple are grown in orchards around the world.

WORD BANK
kernel   single whole grain of a cereal

Glossary

adaptation feature of a living thing that makes it suited to its environment

allele one of a pair of alternative forms of a gene

antibiotic drug used to fight infections caused by bacteria

biodiversity variety of different living things found in a place

breed group of domestic animals with characteristics that distinguish them from other members of the same species

cell the basic unit of life; single cells are the simplest form of life. More complex organisms, such as humans, are made up of trillions of cells.

continuous variation variation that takes place over a range of measurements (for example, height and weight)

discontinuous variation variation in which there are only a few distinct varieties, with nothing in between (for example, blood groups)

dominant gene the allele that determines the appearance, or phenotype, of the organism. For example, if a person has one hair colour allele for brown hair and one for blonde hair, their hair will be brown because brown is the dominant gene.

environment all of the living and non-living things that surround an organism

evolve develop and change over time

extinct describes a species that no longer exists after the last member of the species has died

fertile able to reproduce

fertilization when a sperm cell joins with an egg to make a new cell with two genomes

gene the basic unit of heredity in living things, the means by which characteristics are passed from one generation to the next

genetic engineering deliberately changing the genes of an organism in the laboratory

genetic fingerprinting process of using a person's genetic material to identify them

genome all of the genetic information held in the cells of an organism

genotype the combination of gene pairs (alleles) in an organism with regard to which genes are dominant and which are recessive

heredity the transfer of characteristics from parents to their offspring

hybrid organism that is the offspring of parents from two different species

inherit receive from the previous generation

kernel single whole grain of a cereal

larva (plural: **larvae**) juvenile forms of insects; a maggot is a larva of a fly

mimic take on the appearance of something else

mutate undergo a change in the genes of an organism

mutation gene that has undergone change

nurture all the environmental factors that influence the behaviour and traits of an organism

nutrient substance that living things need in order to survive and grow

obese so overweight that health is endangered

organism any kind of living thing

phenotype appearance of an organism resulting from the interaction between its genes and the environment

protein one of a group of complex chemicals produced by living things to perform tasks such as breaking down food and building cells

recessive gene gene in which the effects are only seen if both alleles in the gene pair are recessive (for example, the gene for blonde hair)

rhesus (Rh) factor a feature of red blood cells that may be present in some people (rhesus positive) and not in others (rhesus negative)

species group of living things that have shared characteristics and which can breed together to produce fertile offspring

subspecies smaller group within a species. A subspecies has some features that set it apart from other members of the species but it is not sufficiently different to be considered as a species in its own right.

World Health Organization the branch of the United Nations that is responsible for dealing with health issues around the world

Find out more

Books

Charles Darwin and the Beagle Adventure, A. J. Wood (Templar Publishing, 2009)

DNA and Heredity, Casey Rand (Heinemann Library, 2010)

Evolution Revolution, Robert Winston (Dorling Kindersley, 2009)

From DNA to GM Wheat, John Farndon (Heinemann Educational Books, 2008)

Genetics: Science in the News, Jenny Vaughan (Franklin Watts, 2008)

Little Lions, Bull Baiters, and Hunting Hounds: A History of Dog Breeds, Jeff Crosby and Sherly Ann Jackson (Tundra Books, 2008)

The Diversity of Species, Michael Bright (Heinemann Library, 2009)

Variation and Classification, Andrew Solway (Heinemann Library, 2006)

What Can We Do About Obesity?, Colin Hynson (Franklin Watts, 2010)

Websites

learn.genetics.utah.edu
Learn Genetics: a wonderfully detailed and comprehensive site with information on genes, heredity, variation, how cells work, and much more.

evolution.berkeley.edu/evolibrary/home.php
Understanding Evolution: described as "your one-stop source for information on evolution". An excellent roundup of ideas on how evolution works.

e360.yale.edu/feature/arctic_roamers_the_move_of_southern_ species_into_far_north/2370
A website with information about grolar bears and other hybrids.

www.nature.com/scitable/topicpage/gregor-mendel-and-the- principles-of-inheritance-593
Find out about Gregor Mendel and his discoveries about inheritance.

www.aboutdarwin.com
Learn more about the life and work of naturalist Charles Darwin.

www.blood.co.uk/about-blood/blood-group-basics
A website with more information about blood groups. This site also describes what happens when someone becomes a blood donor.

Topics to research

Dinovariation

What do we know about variation in living things that lived a long time ago, such as the different types of dinosaurs? They are no longer around so we can't watch them to see if some ran faster than others, or if some had better camouflage, for example. Did natural selection and adaptation work on dinosaurs and other prehistoric living things, just as it has worked on the plants and animals around us today?

Here are a couple of places you could start looking for answers:

paleobiology.si.edu/dinosaurs/index.html

www.mnh.si.edu/exhibits/darwin/carrano.html

Classroom characteristics

How many different ways can you think of that the people in your class at school show variations between each other?

Index